WICKED WRITING SKILLS

OVER 90 NON-FICTION ACTIVITIES

by Lexi Rees

Published in Great Britain
By Outset Publishing Ltd

First edition published September 2020

Written by Lexi Rees
Design by October Creative Ltd

ISBN: 978-1-913799-03-8
www.lexirees.co.uk

How to use this book

This activity book follows on from Creative Writing Skills, which explored the key aspects of fiction writing. In this book, we focus on non-fiction. We will cover opinions, debates, instructions, news, recounts, and marketing. In each section, there are a variety of activities designed to build skills and confidence, plus lots of author tips. The last section is packed with fun non-fiction writing sparks.

Although the activities are grouped into topics, it's not necessary to work through the book in any particular order.

The activities are aimed at children aged seven to eleven but, since there are no right or wrong answers, there's no reason why any child can't have a go, regardless of age or ability.

Warning: there are a few activities that need to be done with friends or family, so you might be asked to join in!

TOP SECRET: FOR AMAZING WRITERS ONLY

Although non-fiction includes FACTS and OPINIONS, it still uses lots of creative writing skills.

Some similarities are:

- it might not have a main character, but it has a main point
- it doesn't have a plot, but it has a structure

Great non-fiction is *persuasive* and *powerful* and could even *change* the world.

In this workbook you're going to learn the top-secret tricks and techniques that:

- businesses use to persuade people to buy their products
- politicians use to persuade people to agree with their views
- journalists use to write articles we want to read

And don't forget, this book is NOT about spelling and punctuation and grammar (although they're obviously great to have in your toolkit). It's about writing wicked non-fiction. It's about making you into an **AMAZING WRITER**.

Let's get started then.

CONTENTS

Chapter one

Outrageous opinions

Everyone loves sharing their opinion, especially when people agree with them. Your job is to make the points clearly, then it's up to the reader (or listener) to decide if they agree or disagree with you.

DID YOU KNOW

You can't be sued for an honestly held opinion? That's why restaurant reviewers and film critics can say things like "*This movie is so boring, you'd better take pyjamas,*" or "*The steak was as tough as shoe leather*".

NOT A LAWYER!

Here's the secret formula for opinion writing:

a clear position + strong arguments = a convincing case

Step 1: State your position on the matter

Don't forget to give the reader a CLUE that it's an opinion in your first line. You could say something like "I think" or "I believe".

Step 2: Build a strong argument

Use facts and examples to back up your opinion. Don't forget to start each new point as a paragraph to make it easy for the reader to follow your logic.

Step 3: Draw your conclusion

Make sure your conclusion packs a powerful punch.

AUTHOR TIP

Even if it's tempting, try not to make up arguments. Hard facts and real examples are far more likely to persuade the reader to agree with you.

Once upon a time

"Once upon a time" is a famous story starter, but it doesn't really work for persuasive writing. Here are some great ways to start writing about your opinion...

I THINK ...

I BELIEVE ...

I FEEL ...

THE BEST ...

MY FAVOURITE ...

IN MY OPINION ...

SPEAKING FOR MYSELF ...

I STRONGLY BELIEVE ...

I OPPOSE ...

FROM MY POINT OF VIEW ...

IT'S MY BELIEF THAT ...

I AM FOR ...

I AM AGAINST ...

I SUPPORT ...

BASED ON MY EXPERIENCE ...

Answer each of these questions using a **different** opener each time.

1. Should everyone learn a foreign language?

2. Should pets be allowed in school?

3. Should it be compulsory to go for a run before work or school?

4. Should weekends be three days long?

5. Should school start earlier?

6. Are self-driving cars dangerous?

7. Does listening to an audio book count as reading?

8. What is the best food?

9. Is pasta good for breakfast?

10. Is social media a waste of time?

SURVIVAL PLAN

Before you start writing, make a list of all the reasons that back up your opinion. Each of these points will become a paragraph.

Make a list of all the things you would need to survive a zombie apocalypse.

To do list
1.
2.
3.

My team members are:
1.
2.
3.

Essential kit
1.
2.
3.

"To survive a zombie apocalypse I would ..."

TIME CONNECTIVES

> ## HEY, I'M A NEW POINT!

Every time you start to write about a new point, make it really clear to the reader this is ANOTHER reason why they should agree with your opinion.

The easiest way to do this is to start a new paragraph using a *logical connective* like one of these to link the points.

First / second / third
First of all
Next
Then
In addition
Additionally
After that
Equally important
Most importantly
Another reason
Besides
Furthermore
And finally

 AUTHOR TIP

Try to group points together under themes to give your argument a much stronger structure.

If I was head teacher for a day, I would

First, _____

_____

_____

_____

Then, _____

_____

_____

_____

After that, _____

_____

_____

_____

And finally, _____

_____

_____

_____

WHO WOULD WIN A RACE BETWEEN A SNAIL AND A WORM?

The _____ would win the race for the following reasons:

Firstly,

Secondly,

In addition,

Furthermore,

WOULD YOU RATHER EAT A <u>RAW ONION</u> OR A <u>LEMON</u>?

Onion ☐ Lemon ☐

REASON 1: ....

....

....

REASON 2: ....

....

....

REASON 3: ....

....

....

REASON 4: ....

....

....

AUTHOR TIP

Try to write a few sentences for each point using FACTS, EXAMPLES and EVIDENCE to support your point.

The EMOTIONAL rollercoaster

Using descriptive adjectives helps the reader picture the strength of your emotions.

a ADMIRABLE, AUTHENTIC

barbarous, bizarre **b**

c CALLOUS, CARELESS

d delightful, dire, dreadful

ENCHANTING, ENJOYABLE, ESSENTIAL, EXTRAVAGANT **e**

f flawed, flimsy, foolish, frivolous

g

GLEAMING, GLOOMY, GROTESQUE

h harmless, heart-breaking, hideous, humdrum

IMAGINATIVE, IMPRACTICAL, INCOMPETENT **i**

jumbled judicious

k KEY, KNOWLEDGEABLE

l lethal, ludicrous

MAGNIFICENT, MEDIOCRE, MONSTROUS **m**

n NECESSARY, NEGLECTED, NOTEWORTHY, NOXIOUS

o obnoxious, obscene, optimistic, outstanding, outrageous

P PATHETIC, PLAUSIBLE, PRODUCTIVE, PROFITABLE, PRUDENT

quaint

quirky

r realistic, reasonable, responsible, ridiculous

SHOCKING, STUNNING, STUPENDOUS

S

t tedious, tenuous, terrible, trustworthy

UGLY, UNFAIR, UNJUST, UNNECESSARY, UNREASONABLE

U

V valuable, vibrant

WONDERFUL, WORST, WORTHWHILE

W

Xenophobic

y young

Z ZEALOUS

MAKE IT **MORE!**

↙ Look at this letter

Dear Sir

An industrial development, located in the national park, has been planned. Your attention is required in order to prevent a blot on the landscape. You must act, or it will be too late. The council is pushing profitability over the environment.

Yours faithfully

A Concerned Citizen

It makes perfect sense, but it's a bit bland. They might even shred your letter without replying! **DON'T PANIC.** We can easily jazz it up by adding these ingredients.

INGREDIENT ONE: *Add some adjectives to show your utter outrage at the proposal. Insert these words into the letter:*

hideous stunning monstrous wonderful

Dear Sir

A ----------- industrial development, located in the --------------- national park, has been planned. Your attention is required in order to prevent a ----------- blot on the landscape. You must act, or it will be too late. The council is pushing profitability over the ----------- environment.

Yours faithfully

recklessly shockingly urgently

Dear Sir

An industrial development ------------- located in the national park, has been planned. Your attention is ------------- required in order to prevent a blot on the landscape. You must act, or it will be too late. The council is ------------- pushing profitability over the environment.

Yours faithfully

---

now immediate still

Dear Sir

An industrial development located in the national park, has been planned. Your ------------- attention is required in order to prevent a blot on the landscape. You must act ------------ ----, or it will be too late. The council is ------------- pushing profitability over the environment.

Yours faithfully

INGREDIENT FOUR: *Sprinkle with adverbs that tell you WHERE things happen. These all relate to places e.g. everywhere, nowhere, inside, outside... Insert these words into the letter:*

everywhere heart

Dear Sir

An industrial development located in the --------------- of the national park, has been planned. Your attention is required in order to prevent a blot on the landscape. You must act, or it will be too late. The council is pushing profitability over the environment --------------- .

Yours faithfully

INGREDIENT FIVE: *Garnish with adverbs that tell you TO WHAT EXTENT things happen. These measure the scale. "Very" is the most common adverb in this category. Insert these words into the letter:*

outrageous really

Dear Sir

An --------------- industrial development located in the of the national park, has been planned. Your attention is --------------- required in order to prevent a blot on the landscape. You must act, or it will be too late. The council is pushing profitability over the environment.

Yours faithfully

NOW, STIR THEM ALL TOGETHER

Dear Sir

An ----------, ---------- industrial development ---------- located in the ---------- of the national park, has been planned. Your ------------- attention is ---------- required ---------- in order to prevent a blot on the landscape. You must act ----------, or it will be too late. The council is ----------, ---------- pushing profitability over the environment ----------.

Yours faithfully
A Concerned Citizen

Do you think this is more persuasive?

Yes ☐   No ☐

WRAP IT UP

Although the reader should be in no doubt about your opinion by now, you still need a slam-dunk conclusion. Don't trail off with "And so, err, that's kind of all I had to say." Instead, try to use a strong phrase.

Go back through your answers to the exercises you've done so far and tick which of these endings you used

☐ For all these reasons...

☐ Consequently...

☐ Clearly...

☐ Obviously...

☐ Finally...

☐ As you can see...

☐ To summarise...

☐ To sum up...

☐ In conclusion...

Which do you think is more POWERFUL, the wind or the sea?

Don't forget to include

- a clear opening statement
- several different reasons, each starting with a clear marker
- evidence to back up your reasons
- a killer conclusion

Who would win a spelling bee, alphabetti spaghetti or a computer keyboard?

Could we end disease?

WHAT WOULD HAPPEN IF FOOTBALL HAD NEVER BEEN INVENTED?

Convince your parents to buy you the latest mobile phone.

Do we all see colour the same way?

_____

_____

_____

_____

_____

_____

_____

_____

_____

_____

_____

_____

IS FANTASY BETTER THAN REAL LIFE?

ARE HUMANS MORE IMPORTANT THAN PLANTS?

Can you make your own luck?

Dynamite debates

In a debate, you're tackling a statement rather than a question. Debates are like a tug of war with the one team being FOR and the other team AGAINST.

> Opinion writing will start this way
> **"ARE VIDEO GAMES BAD FOR YOU?"**
>
> In a debate, the same topic would be phrased like this
> **"VIDEO GAMES ARE BAD FOR YOU."**

This statement is sometimes called a MOTION.

Debate Rules

- ☑ Use formal language
- ☑ Consider alternative points of view
- ☑ Organise the arguments using lists headed For and Against
- ☑ Spend some time researching facts and gathering evidence
- ☑ Don't present opinions as facts
- ☑ It is never acceptable to be rude or aggressive

How many arguments can you think of for this debate?

Plastic should be banned in supermarkets.

FOR	AGAINST

AUTHOR TIP

Try not to use words like **"ALWAYS"** or **"NEVER"** as the opposition can easily pick holes in those statements.

The Great Balloon DEBATE

You're in a hot air balloon but it's losing height.
SOMEONE HAS TO JUMP OFF TO SAVE THE OTHERS.

who do you choose...?

You'll need to do this activity with your friends or family.

Choose one of these groups (or make up your own). Allocate each person a character from that list.

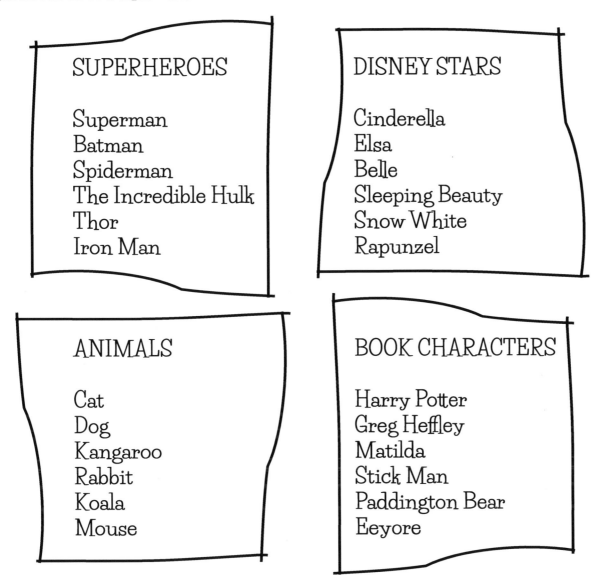

SUPERHEROES

Superman
Batman
Spiderman
The Incredible Hulk
Thor
Iron Man

DISNEY STARS

Cinderella
Elsa
Belle
Sleeping Beauty
Snow White
Rapunzel

ANIMALS

Cat
Dog
Kangaroo
Rabbit
Koala
Mouse

BOOK CHARACTERS

Harry Potter
Greg Heffley
Matilda
Stick Man
Paddington Bear
Eeyore

HOW TO PLAY

Take turns to give ONE reason why you must stay in the balloon.
After everyone has presented their case, do a secret vote on who should jump.
The person with the most votes must leap overboard.

If two or more characters get an equal number of votes, they have to present again and another vote is held. Keep going until there is only one person left.
NOTE: you must give a different reason every time you speak.

" Everyone over the age of ten should be able to vote. **"**

Do you agree or disagree with this statement. Why?

OFFICIAL VOTING SLIP

"People should pass a test before they can own a dog."

Write an argument to support this statement.

_____

_____

_____

_____

_____

_____

_____

_____

_____

_____

_____

_____

_____

_____

_____

_____

_____

_____

It should be illegal to use a car without taking passengers.

School holidays are a waste of valuable learning time.

Too much money makes you unhappy...

Children should donate 10% of any pocket money to charity.

FOR	AGAINST

Oink!

HAVE A LIVE DEBATE!

You'll need to do this with your friends or family.

Rules
- Split into two teams.
- Spend a few minutes preparing your arguments.
- Each speaker gets three minutes to present their case.
- The other team cannot interrupt during a speech.

"The question we are considering is ..."

A RHINO WOULD BEAT AN ELEPHANT IN A GAME OF TUG OF WAR.

FOR Team Members

AGAINST Team Members

READY, STEADY, GO!

"We will now take a vote."

Who won?

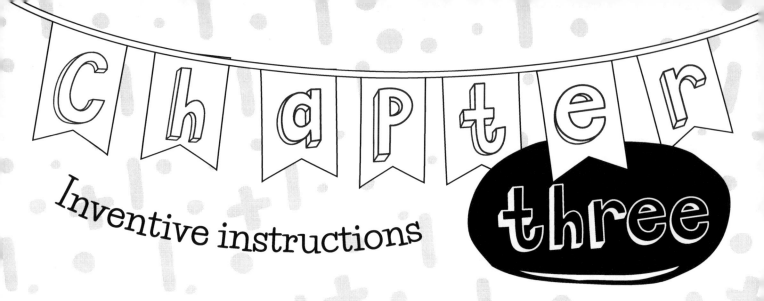

Inventive instructions

Chapter three

Have you ever tried to bake a cake and it was a disaster? If the instructions are clear, every cake would look and taste exactly the same.

CHEF:

"Stir the mixture."

ME:

"For how long? What with? HELP!"

Here are the ingredients for a good set of instructions:

- List any materials required at the start
- Keep each step short and clear
- Make sure the order is logical
- Use headings and subheadings
- Separate the steps with bullet points, numbers, markers, or time connectives (e.g. first, then, next).

HOW TO CATCH A DRAGON

EQUIPMENT:

STEPS:

1.

2.

3.

4.

5.

6.

HOW TO SURVIVE IN THE JUNGLE

EQUIPMENT:

STEPS:

1.

2.

3.

4.

5.

6.

HOW WOULD YOU TEACH AN ALIEN TO SWIM?

EQUIPMENT:

STEPS:

1. -------------------------------- 4. --------------------------------

2. -------------------------------- 5. --------------------------------

3. -------------------------------- 6. --------------------------------

Explain how to use social media to your
GREAT-GREAT-GREAT GRANDMOTHER

Equipment:

Steps:

1.

2.

3.

4.

5.

6.

Tell me more about Tik-Tok dear...

THE NEW BABYSITTER ARRIVES BUT YOUR PARENTS FORGOT TO GIVE THEM ANY INSTRUCTIONS!

WRITE A MANUAL.

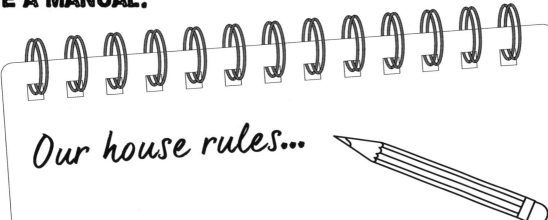

Our house rules...

HOW DO YOU BUILD AN EGYPTIAN PYRAMID?

EQUIPMENT:

STEPS:

1.

2.

3.

4.

5.

6.

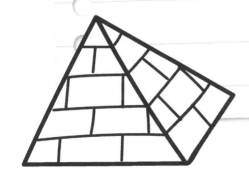

INVENT A NEW SPORT

MY SPORT IS CALLED:

TO PLAY YOU WILL NEED:

>

>

>

RULES:

1.

2.

3.

4.

5.

SCORING + HOW TO WIN:

Chapter four

Nuclear news

Whether it is printed or online, the news is read by millions of people every day. Here are the ingredients for a great article:

- Include an attention-grabbing headline
- Always write in the third person, (he/ she) not the first person (I)
- Use the past tense
- Interview people and add quotes
- Photos need captions
- Cover each of the 5 W's:

Who, What, Why, Where, When

AUTHOR TIP

Put the most important points first (newspapers are often only skim read).

HIT THE HEADLINES

Newspaper headlines are very short - normally only a few words.

CATWOMAN SAVES DOG

HIKER SURVIVES BEAR ATTACK

SUMMER FAIR CANCELLED

DID YOU KNOW? THE HEADLINE IS USUALLY WRITTEN BY A COPY EDITOR, NOT THE REPORTER.

Column space is very limited and the editor knows the maximum number of characters that will fit on a row. Each row of a headline is called a "deck". Sometimes the headline is split over two rows. Journalists call this a "two-deck headline".

Here is a two-deck headline with character counts of 14 and 19:

COWS LOSE JOBS
AS MILK PRICES FALL

AUTHOR TIP

Spaces between words and punctuation count as characters.

QUESTION TIME

News articles should answer THE FIVE Ws
who, what, where, when, and why

Example

WHO

WHAT

WHERE

WHEN

A **tiger escaped** from **London zoo last night** after a lightning strike cut the power to the electric fences. Police have closed central London and residents are requested to **stay indoors** until it is found.

WHY

Find an interesting article, cut it out, and stick it in here. Now underline the answers to these questions.

WHO IS THE ARTICLE ABOUT?
WHAT HAPPENED?
WHERE DID IT HAPPEN?
WHEN DID IT HAPPEN?
WHY IS IT IMPORTANT?

[ARTICLE GOES HERE]

AUTHOR TIP

Because people often skim read newspapers, the story should put the most important/interesting W first. For example, if the tiger article above started with "A lightning strike caused a power cut" you might not read on. The escaped tiger is much more newsworthy.

ALL THE SOCKS IN THE WORLD HAVE VANISHED.

Write a newspaper article about this terrifying situation.
Include a headline with no more than 20 characters.
(Don't forget to count the spaces as well as the letters.)

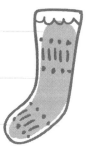

A celebrity lives in your town. Their cat is kidnapped and they get a ransom note. Write an article for your local newspaper.

Local News

CATNAPPED!

FIND AN OLD NEWSPAPER.
CUT OR PRINT OUT YOUR FAVOURITE
HEADLINES AND STICK THEM IN HERE.

[HEADLINE GOES HERE]

How many decks are there? ....
How many characters are there per deck? ....

[HEADLINE GOES HERE]

How many decks are there? ....
How many characters are there per deck? ....

[HEADLINE GOES HERE]

How many decks are there? ....
How many characters are there per deck? ....

[HEADLINE GOES HERE]

How many decks are there? ....
How many characters are there per deck? ....

AUTHOR TIP

In headlines, words are often removed without changing the meaning, even if it makes the grammar a little bit wonky.

The scientists discover a cure

becomes

Scientists Discover Cure

BY THE BYLINE

The byline is your name. It's usually added beneath the headline.

BEAR HUNT

by Lexi Rees

Just like you recognise author names, if you read a newspaper regularly, you will start to look out for stories by your favourite journalists.

 AUTHOR TIP

As an alternative, you could add your byline into the end of the first paragraph like this:

Police search the woods for a teddy bear reported to be stealing picnics, *writes Lexi Rees, Crime Desk.*

Write a report about a crime.
Don't forget to include a HEADLINE and your BYLINE.

crime report

"DON'T Quote ME ON THAT..."

Interview techniques are one of the first things a journalist is taught. A great quote can lift a story from average to awesome.

Find a newspaper article with several quotes in it. Cut or print it out and stick it here. Underline all the quotes.

How many quotes did the journalist use?

1 ☐ 2 ☐ 3 ☐ More than 4 ☐

Why do you think they chose those people to be interviewed?

AUTHOR TIP

Always ask permission if you're going to quote someone.

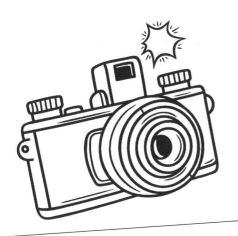

Snap!

Not every newspaper article has a picture with it, but the editor will always be pleased if you can offer them a photo too.

If you're including a photo, remember to:

- credit the photographer by including their name,
- add a cool caption under the picture.

AUTHOR TIP
Images belong to the photographer. This is called copyright. If you want to publish a picture you didn't take yourself, you need permission. The law is complicated, so don't get into trouble!

Find some newspaper pictures and look at the captions. Stick your favourites here:

Add your own captions to these sketches

- -

- - - - - - your own captions to these sketches -

It's all in the BRAND

What would you call your newspaper?

- -

Once you've decided the name, you need to design a MASTHEAD. This is the title (in a really cool font) and a logo, and is positioned at the top of the front page.

YOUR LOGO & TITLE

Publish your own newspaper.

You'll need paper and pens to complete this.
Try this with your friends or family.

- NAME YOUR PUBLICATION
- DESIGN THE MASTHEAD
- SET THE PRICE
- ALLOCATE JOBS TO EACH PERSON

Editor   ----------------------------------

News correspondent   ----------------------------------

Sports reporter   ----------------------------------

Gossip columnist   ----------------------------------

Agony aunt   ----------------------------------

Games reviewer   ----------------------------------

Astrologer (writes horoscopes) ----------------------------------

- WRITE THE ARTICLES
- STICK THEM TOGETHER

BOOM
You just published your first newspaper!

You are now officially a journalist.

Does fake news matter?

As a journalist, your job is to report the news. What could you do to make sure your stories aren't 'fake news'?

*Fake news is deliberate misinformation or hoaxes, and is easily spread via social media.

Chapter five

Tell-tale time

Reports of events are called "recounts". These can be in a diary, journal, report, or a newspaper.

Here are the ingredients for a recount:

- Follow events in the order they happened
- Use the past tense
- Write in the first person (I) for diaries and journals
- Write in the third person (he/she) for newspaper reports

AUTHOR TIP

Use specific time references: day, date, time, morning/afternoon/evening, before breakfast, after school, etc.

TOP SECRET

Everyone knows you shouldn't read someone else's diary BUT we're all really nosy and we LOVE secrets.

That's why diaries and journals are so interesting to read.

HAVE YOU READ ANY OF THESE?

1. **Diary of a Wimpy Kid** ☐

2. **Dork Diaries** ☐

3. **Anne Frank's diary** ☐

4. **The Secret Diary of Adrian Mole** ☐

5. **The Brilliant World of Tom Gates** ☐

Have you read any other books written as a private diary or journal?

Dear Diary

Monday

Tuesday

Wednesday

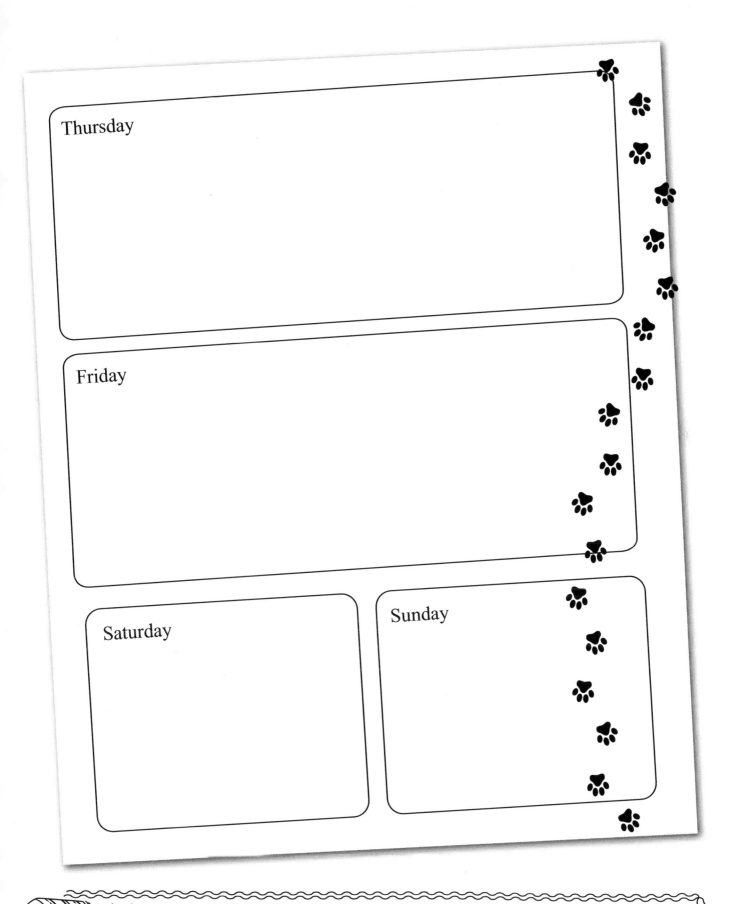

Thursday

Friday

Saturday

Sunday

"I'M SPEECHLESS!"

Draw a picture that sums up what happened to you. Annotate each drawing with a time marker e.g. during break, after school, at dinner, after lights out.

Monday

Tuesday

Wednesday

Thursday

Friday

Saturday

Sunday

Write a report about a sports match.

Write a report about

A DAY IN THE LIFE OF A SOLDIER

Write a police report of a murder, chronologically recording all the events in the run up to the body being discovered.

POLICE LINE DO NOT CROSS

POLICE LINE DO NOT CROSS

POLICE LINE DO NOT CROSS

POLICE LINE DO NOT CROSS

 # Write an email to a friend
telling them about your holiday

New message ___ □ ×

To

Subject

Send

Chapter

Marketing mayhem

SiX

Every day, we're bombarded with companies trying to persuade us to buy their products. Here are the ingredients for a great advert.

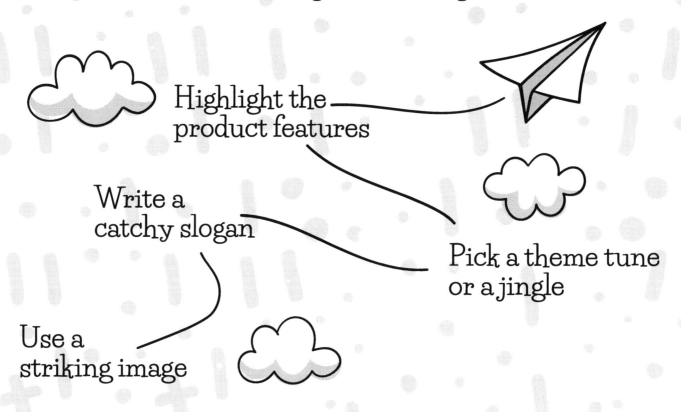

Highlight the product features

Write a catchy slogan

Pick a theme tune or a jingle

Use a striking image

AUTHOR TIP

Before you start to design an advert, you need to identify the *target market*. An advert targeting gardeners will look very different to one targeting gamers.

 # ADVERT AWARDS

Make a list of the best adverts you've ever seen. What made them so good?

1. _____

2. _____

3. _____

4. _____

5. _____

6. _____

7. _____

8. _____

Now ask your friends and family about the adverts they remember most clearly. Are they different to your choices?

```



```

Draw a poster to advertise a dog show. You must include:

(1) How to enter   (2) When and where it is   (3) Prizes

WANTED

★★★★★

DEAD OR ALIVE

REWARD

YOU'RE SETTING UP A BAND. DESIGN A POSTER FOR THE AUDITIONS.

CATCH PHRASE!

Lots of companies and products use a short, catchy tagline or slogan. The best taglines are instantly associated with a brand or product. How many of these do you recognise?

Slogan	Brand/Product
JUST DO IT	_____
FINGER LICKIN' GOOD	_____
I'M LOVIN' IT	_____
SNAP! CRACKLE! POP!	_____
HAVE A BREAK, HAVE A	_____
MELTS IN YOUR MOUTH, NOT IN YOUR HANDS	_____
MAYBE SHE'S BORN WITH IT. MAYBE IT'S	_____
ONCE YOU POP, YOU CAN'T STOP	_____

Can you think of any others?

_____

_____

PINEAPPLE PERSUASION

Plan the storyboard for an advert starring a hedgehog with hair that sticks up so it looks like a pineapple. You can choose what product it is advertising. Don't forget to feature the brand and tagline somewhere in the advert.

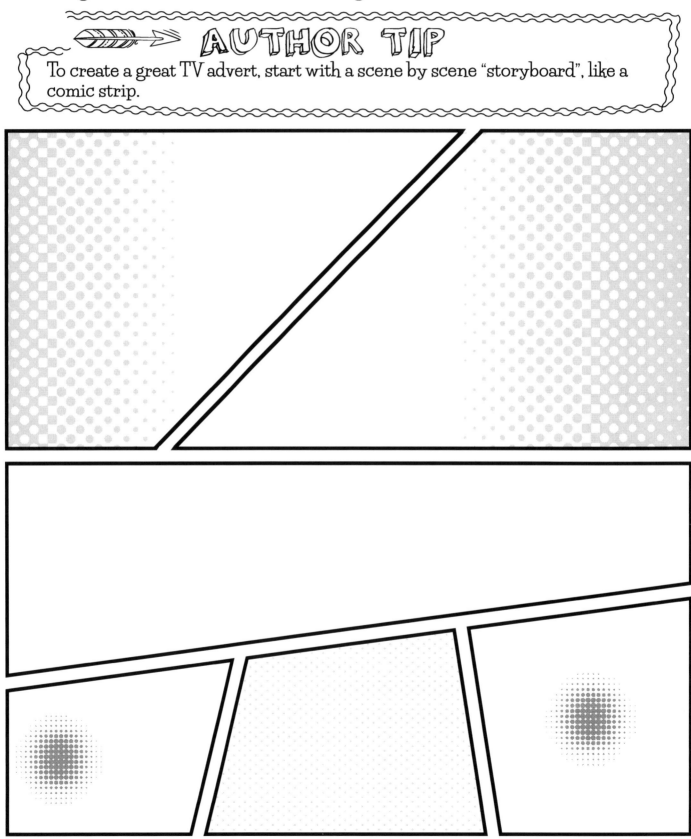

DESIGN A LEAFLET FOR A PIZZA DELIVERY COMPANY

Don't forget to include the pizza name, product number, price and a short description.

Chapter seven

Wicked writing sparks

Would you rather live in the jungle or the desert?

OPINION

Is life easier for birds or fish?

WOULD IT BE EASIER TO TEACH A CAT OR A DOG TO SKI?

OPINION

Which came first
SUMMER OR WINTER?

OPINION

_____
_____
_____
_____
_____
_____
_____
_____
_____
_____

Who would win a battle between *zombies* and *ghosts*?

Which came first,

the CAPITAL LETTER **A** or the small letter **a**?

Which came first, the Easter Egg or the Easter Bunny?

OPINION

WHICH CAME FIRST, ALIENS OR HUMANS?

Putting a mirror next to a candle in a dark room means you now have twice as much light.

DEBATE

BIRTHDAY CAKES SHOULD BE BANNED AT SCHOOL.

E-GAMING IS A SPORT.

DEBATE

It's okay to be mean to a bully.

DEBATE

You should say "PLEASE" and "thank you" to a robot.

A twin is never alone...

Do we stay the same from birth?

DEBATE

Would it be better if we all spoke the same language?

How to construct an award-winning ice sculpture.

Equipment

Steps

1.

2.

3.

4.

5.

6.

INSTRUCTIONS

How to interview a police suspect.

Newsflash!

It's the week before Christmas and Santa Claus's reindeer have gone on strike. Write an article for your newspaper. Don't forget to include:

- an attention-grabbing headline
- your byline
- at least one quote
- an image with a cool caption

NEWSPAPER

FRONT PAGE NEWS

You're interviewing rescue workers and evacuees after one of these events: - *A BUSHFIRE* – *A TSUNAMI* – *A TORNADO*

NEWSPAPER

Write an article for your newspaper.

DOUBLE TROUBLE

Journalists often use alliteration in their headlines to make an impact. Here are some headlines:

TRAMP TRIUMPHS

CHARLIE CHARGED

Can you find any other examples? Copy or stick them in here.

PLAY WITH PUNS

Another headline trick is to use puns, twisting the words. Here are some examples:

HUNGRY HAMBURGLAR

CARS STUCK IN JAM

Can you find any other examples? Copy or stick them in here.

A day in the life of an astronaut

RECOUNT

I couldn't do my homework last night because when I got home...

$$\sqrt{\frac{3R_mT}{M_R 10^{-3}}} \quad P = \frac{E}{C} = \frac{hf}{C} = \frac{h}{\lambda} \quad V = V_1(1 + \beta \Delta t)$$

Design a poster to show people how to stop *disease* from spreading.

Plan the storyboard to advertise a new game.

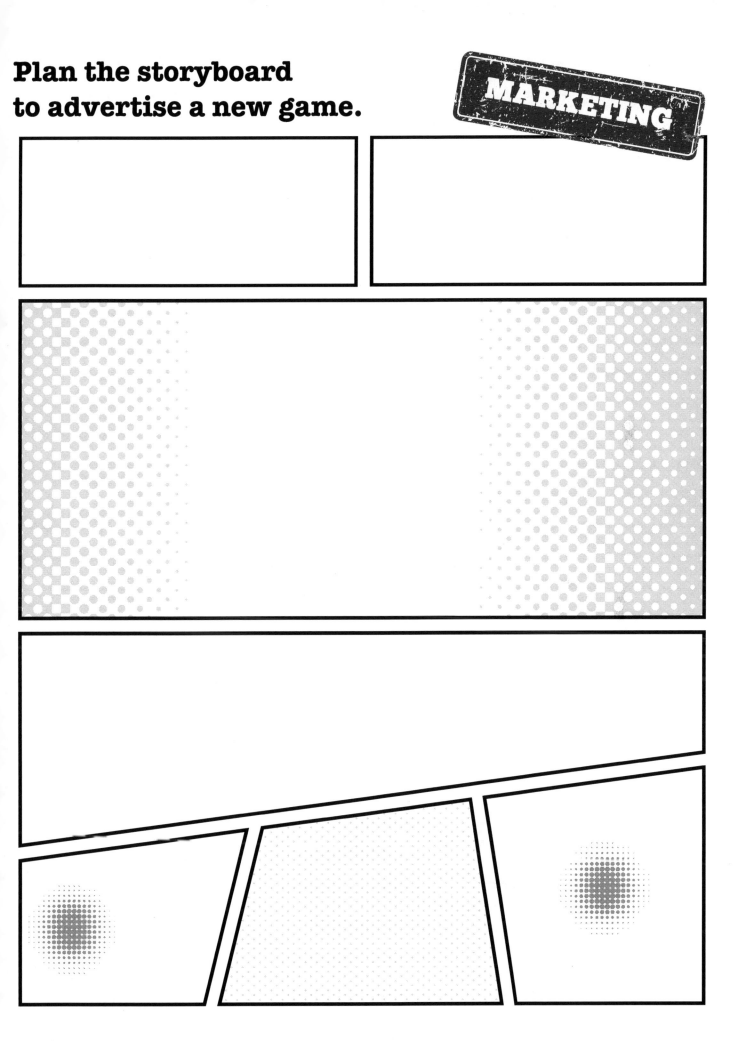

DESIGN A CATALOGUE FOR ONE OF THE FOLLOWING:

a clothes shop / a toy shop / a flower shop / a holiday company

MARKETING

If you enjoyed this book, please tell your friends!

You might like to subscribe to my free newsletter. Here's what you can expect from it:

- fun writing activities and puzzles
- exclusive author interviews
- recommendations for cool books
- details of any special promotions and new book releases

You can find out more here:
www.lexirees.co.uk/kidsclub

Happy reading!

Lexi

ABOUT THE AUTHOR

Lexi Rees grew up in the north of Scotland but now splits her time between London and West Sussex.

She's usually covered in straw or glitter, and frequently both.

GET IN TOUCH

If you have any questions, you can contact me via my website www.lexirees.co.uk or on social media.

🐦 @lexi_rees

f @LexiAuthor

⬚ @lexi.rees

Look forward to chatting,
Lexi

Also by the Author:

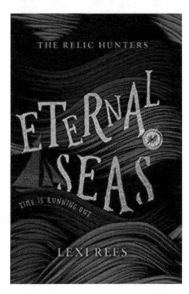

Made in the USA
Las Vegas, NV
11 June 2023

73274021R00070